words to fit thoughts

poems by
n. a. welhoelter

Acorn Press   Austin, Texas

TO
SNOOKIE
MY DARLING WIFE
with love

My thanks and appreciation
to my daughter Mollie, who
produced these pages from
my scribblings.

If you find yourself anywhere
in this book, I am pleased.

n. a. welhoelter

Second Edition

© 1992 by N. A. Welhoelter

Copyright © under the Universal Copyright
and Berne Conventions

ISBN 0-682-48602-7

Printed in the United States of America

CONTENTS

CONTENTS

CONTENTS

CONTENTS

CONTENTS

CONTENTS

CONTENTS

CONTENTS

CONTENTS

CONTENTS

unpaid

good poets never sell a verse
they all die poor and thin
they're in caskets six feet under
when the royalties come in

that stuff

there are things i write and make
that thrill me to the core
but they will be of little worth
when i am here no more
unless you like it very much
please hear me while i say
don't clutter up your place for me
just throw the stuff away

snookie

there's blue in her eyes
there is silver in her hair
there's a smile upon her lips
she spreads gladness everywhere

she is neat she's trim and pretty
she's as true as true can be
she's the greatest thing that's happened
to her daughters and to me

your book

fun in life is what you do
and most of what you say
practice your remembering
so you'll recall someday
all the bits and pieces
you can instantly replay

relive your life a thousand times
as time slips quietly by
as practice makes you perfect
you will build a good supply
a storybook that's all your own
that helps you laugh and cry

my jesus hanging there

do you see my jesus hanging there
against his darkened sky
this morning's blood still clinging loose
the sweat won't let it dry

see there a newly opened wound
let's run a crimson streak
the salt the sweat the dirt and blood
burn hot his eyes-now weak

do you see my jesus hanging there
as his lightning lights his face
see any signs of mercy-
coming down-or in this place

see drops of blood beneath his cross
stain red his earth he made
and widen out in seas of love
'til every debt is paid

do you see my jesus hanging there
could you now commit one sin
because my jesus hangs there-
heaven's open-please go in

maryann

my daddy wrote this poem
when i was a little tot
he said i was eleven weeks
in case i e'er forgot

he said my hair was golden
and i had the cutest curl
my mother used to fix it-
she was glad i was a girl

i used to twist my little head
and look with much surprise
at everything about me
with a pair of big blue eyes

i took my milk and orange juice
without a bit of trouble
and it made me very happy
when my tummy lost its bubble

people walking 'round didn't
bother me-i slept so sound
but if i made the slightest noise
to my crib they'd bound

we surely were a happy lot
my dad and me and mother
and no matter what else happens
we will always love each other

mother's day

we are so awful little
we don't know what to say
so daddy said he'd write some lines
'cause this is mother's day
he said you work so hard for us
but that you do not mind
just so that we love you
and our happiness we'll find
we do love you dear mother
but not just this mother's day
we loved you all the days that passed
and those yet far away

maryann starts to school
september 3, 1944

her baby days have slipped away
for she must start to school today
we taught her how to eat and walk
we taught her how to dress and talk
we taught her how to be polite
we taught her what was wrong and right
but there are other things to know
so off to school our tot must go
she looks so little as she goes
to meet a world of trials and woes
we watch her start with joy and tears
we now to guide her through the years.

nancy

my daddy wrote this poem when i was a tiny tot
he said i was just seven weeks in case i e'er forgot
he said my hair was rather dark and quite far down my neck
he said that i was one fine girl and bragged of it-by heck

he told the folks all up and down that i was good as gold
i had many other attributes-too many to unfold
he said my greatest attribute was majoring in sleep
they'd put me in my little bed and never hear a peep

he said i used to wet so much-but mother kept me clean
she did not have to wring so much-she had a wash machine
there was my formula-of course-which had to cook an hour
which among some other things contained some barley flour

my great big sister maryann was then 'tween two and three
it used to really tickle her to pet cute little me
mother did not mind the work and daddy helped her too
i guess with all the four of us was quite a bit to do

we had fun and trouble in the days of nineteen forty
we would laugh and cry together-we were young and mighty hearty
we surely were a happy lot us kids our dad and mother
and no matter what else happens we will always love each other

mother's children

dressing up their dollies little girlies
    just adore
or they pull out all of mother's stuff
    and play they have a store
or they cook out in the kitchen
    with their little pots and pans
and they mess the place up awful
    with their sticky little hands

mother picks up doll-dress scraps
    and gathers up her stuff
she wipes the kitchen walls where
    sticky hands have made them rough
no matter what the girlies do
    mother always takes their part
and if anyone offended them
    'twould break their mother's heart

but let a boy try some of that
    and see how far he gets
if he digs a cave out in the yard
    he always has regrets
if he accidentally kicks a football
    through a windowpane
it's a long time 'fore he's able
    to kick at one again

if he does his acrobatics
    on his mother's featherbed
she takes him for a visit
    out into the shed
tho mother does not show it
    she is doing all she can
to raise her girl a lady
    and her little boy a man

sally

my daddy wrote this poem
when i was fully grown
i had two sons and bearing
if the truth were known
made writing hard to seek the past
those incidences of joy
that stretch from days i can recall
to "is it girl or boy"
oh i remember-so does he
the days we knew so well
i saw him hammer, saw, and nail
and roller skate dare tell
i was daddy's shadow
no matter what he did
i handed him his tools and things
when just a little kid
then down along the way somewhere
we had to step apart
when little girls get bigger
they have to play the part
my years have taught me many things
too many to relate
especially many happy things
that happened here of late
we surely were a happy lot
us kids our dad and mother
and no matter what else happens
we will always love each other

no statue please

i don't want to leave a statue
of me standing in the square
'cause halloween will dress me
and there's lots of pigeons there

i'd like to leave some little things
to last for years to come
like "i know 'cause daddy told me"
and the songs i like to hum

my whistle should go down with time
it's tuned to many ears
and i think i've done some funny things
that might last through the years

but the thing i really hope will last
and linger big and tall
is that i was a happy man
and that i loved you all

mollie

my daddy wrote this poem
while i was away at school
by then i was a young adult
and i was really cool
i had long hair and pretty teeth
my eyes could sparkle clear
i could sing the dumbest song
i had a music ear
i had a boy and he was fine
he'd been approved by all
he was polite and thoughtful
and oh yes he was tall
my studies had exotic names
my books were big and thick
i exercised and shot a bow
and that was quite a trick
i cried a bit and had two fish
did things like other girls
looked a mess on rising
and when done up in curls
but i was kind of pretty
when dressed and fixed to go
daddy'd say "you're pretty"
and that's the way i'd know
we surely were a happy lot
us girls our dad and mother
and no matter what else happens
we will always love each other

rancho amigo

guadalupe river rippling by
looks up against the texas sky
between these on the highest hill
is rancho amigo the dreamer's thrill
kissed by rainbows and southern sun
this paradise in stone is spun
a cheery comfort reigns within
there is no heart its charm can't win

your storms

when the clouds top the horizon
and they peak in thunderheads
when the thunder sends no message
and the lightning looks like threads

then's the time to take precautions
and to formulate a plan
to protect the things you cherish
in the best way that you can

then brace and meet the menace
with confidence and prayer
so when the storm is over
you and yours will still be there

terri

my daddy wrote this poem
when i was just sixteen
far beyond a little girl
a little short of queen
i did my thing as normally
as any sixteen-year-old would
'cause i was what i ought to be
and that is what is good
i lived each minute to the brim
between each joy and sorrow
many things i could not bear
and prayed for each tomorrow
for then i'd be much older
and wiser too i knew
and folks would understand me
and the things i do
oh there was ecstasy galore
a car-a phone-a boy
a pretty room-a dollar bill
and more to bring me joy
like bathing-primping-laughing
records-earrings-beads
someone seemed to furnish
all my many needs
we surely were a happy lot
us kids our dad and mother
and no matter what else happens
we will always love each other

my eternal existence

certainly there'll be a change
from things as they are now
for if I am to live forever
I'll be rearranged somehow

i'll go along the way i am
a body and a soul
the body makes decisions
as it plods to reach its goal

carefully i plan each move
take heed of every breath-
but the goal is what's confusing
for there is no goal but death

oh yes i see-past death i "live"
so in eternity
death is just the second thing
that happened "unto" me

it's the third thing that's important
it's the "where" will i exist
I can have no less than heaven
if only i insist

what is love?

what is love well i don't know
i'll explain as best i can
it's invisible stuff like ether
that dwells in the heart of man
it's the thing that makes mothers suffer so
it makes children cry out in the night
it's the thing that builds the family
it's what urges men to fight
it's a thing that kills and murders
it brings kisses too and tears
it's the thing that heals the wounded
it builds courage sometimes fears
it's expensive yet the cheapest thing
it's the greatest gift to give
it's the thing that makes us want to die
yet makes us want to live

trust

you who hold the reins beware
we follow you in haste
you should know where we may go
pray lead us not to waste
we heed your call to do the task
if it be large or small
resolve with care be just and fair
for you decide for all

not dead

i pulled a dead blossom
from a plant one day
i was just about
to throw it away
when the sight of some seeds
stayed in my hand
and i think i heard
a slight command
so i put the seeds
upon the ground
and later on
i came around
several blossoms
bowed with grace
as they adorned
their little place
"nice" i said
and swelled with pride
and i felt good
down deep inside

time tested

she's not the girl you married
and he's not the boy you knew
the love you have is better
reborn each day anew

fresh yet with experience
tempered too by age
tuned to understanding
tenderness and sage

i'll never tell

coveted are the secrets
of the working of the mind
millions of ideas flashing
things of every kind
and you say "i know you"
and i sometimes say the same
when if you knew what i was thinking
'twould really be a shame
it takes some great contortion
to control my smiling face
when my heart is near to breaking
in this sad and tearful case
no one knows you-no one knows me
each is one alone
'tis the only thing that's private
sacred and your own

want a family tree

if you want a family tree
with branches and roots real strong
you will have to start it early
and let it grow real long

it isn't something that you can buy
or work out late in life
you do not get it without pain
or a bundle of tears and strife

but the pain is far outweighed
by the faces the smiles and fun
and the glory you reap in doing
what you dreamed of when you begun

boo

there's a goblin at the window
and the wind is howling loud
there are ghosts in every corner
as i dress up in my shroud

this is the night i scare folks
i'm ghastly, gray, and lean
i'll be busy till tomorrow
i'm the ghost of halloween

my dad

very few people knew my dad
he was quiet and seemed alone
he seldom spoke and when he did
his words were few and soft in tone
because of his work he was seldom home
at regular hours-that is
he worked backstage in theaters
those strange hours of-show biz
he hummed a lot and could whistle good
a thousand or so songs i guess
from modern tunes to opera
tin pan and "porgy and bess"
he could fix anything-make things from scratch
he could paint and plant things to grow
he did not drive nor did he care
the bus went where he wanted to go
he did not like barbers who talked a lot
and went clear across town to be sure
he was neat as a pin-dressed it too
could appear quite rich-when poor
he was handsome-his hair was silver and waved
i doubt he had all the things that he wished
but he never revealed what he craved
he showed up at church for weddings and things
and we all went to catholic schools
i'm sure that he prayed and understood why
but he lived by his own set of rules
that's all i remember-that's not very much
but i really did not know my dad
i'm sure there must be lots more to tell
that i know so little-is sad

depression

we are making history
for students to consume
the subject is depression
and the outlook is a boom

if we treat the subject right
the end will be sublime
and depression will be history
right here in our own time

so let's all get together
and figure this thing out
we've done bigger things and
we'll do this without a doubt

problems

some problems have many solutions
others have very few
those problems with many are easy
the others are hard to do
all problems tend to change things
which goes against the grain
especially when the changes
result in tears and pain

try this

leave all the doors wide open
never lock or slam
level paths through mountains
never build a dam
drench not the view
with floods of tears
or turn a deafened ear
let love and wisdom enter
to minimize the fear

"ambitious"

the question of the unemployed
has caused the country grief
a lot of poor unfortunates
are living on relief

some are living on their folks
and others on their wits
what think you of a normal man
who has a job and quits

now

happiness is words and acts
expressed by those who care
performed most anytime at all
with eagerness to share

let others know your inner thoughts
don't hold back words of praise
of love or little compliments
that make for joyful days

don't wait until the final hour
or 'til the curfew blows
to tell the things you just assume
the other fellow knows

friendship lost

little by little the ties slip away
and even tho it must be so
it's hard to watch them slowly go
'til the thing is over passed and gone
like the still of night that has no dawn
there's nothing that can take its place
nothing left you must erase
it's empty-gone-released and naught
a lesson learned a lesson taught

defense

out of the earth comes the ore
off of the scrap heap the steel
into a mold to make cannon
into another for wheel
aluminum out of the kitchen
for airplanes that fly and spin
scientists labor for hours
to defeat the shortage of tin
legs must go back into cotton
cocoons are nourished with care
silk must go to the army
for weapons of land and air
sweat must pour from brow of man
his muscles must ripple with speed
leaders must be diplomatic
for time is another great need
we must put in our share of money
for times are very tense
america lives in the future
only with proper defense

"mail from home"

the best thing that i've ever seen
since i started out to roam
is a bit of mail to tell me
what is going on back home

it makes no difference either
if they're short or if they're long
just so it's news of you back there
the words are like a song

don't wait so long to tell me
how you feel and what you do
'cause if i don't get mail from home
i'm sad and mighty blue

"average americans"
(1940)

we're the average american family -
two kids, we rent, have a car
i smoke lots of cigarettes
and now and then a cigar

my wife does the washing and ironing
by herself she prepares all the meals
together we wash up the dishes
my old shoes get half-soles and heels

i make the fire in the morning
i go out to work about eight
now and then we go to a party -
very seldom do we stay out late

we pay for our ice-box in dribbles
and balance the budget near red
we work, play and sleep in a wonderful land
'tis the best in the world it is said.

me-my-mine

i work and i sweat-i fuss
and i pine
over what's gonna happen
to me-my-mine
i gather in people
and various things
for the sake of possession
and pleasure it brings
i'm jealous and proud
to the point of disgrace
i want what is mine
in its own little place
my possessions intrigue me
they glitter and shine
this world around me
is me-my-mine

the war

war years are slipping painfully by
rushed along by battle cry
we waited for war clouds to break
saw europe tremble in their wake
little countries soon dropped out
france collapsed-we thought her stout
london toppled but she held
norway crashed as trees were felled
greece then fell and likewise crete
russia turned a near defeat
pearl harbor could not suffer more
the british lost at singapore
little islands one by one
fell before the mighty gun
the fate of all was on the scale
the future dim-the chances frail
but as history shows us-once again
right prevails and ends the pain

our larry

he's still the larry we once knew
who needs soles upon each shoe.

who drove the car, with one pane out,
that made dogs bark and kids to shout.

the self same one, that lived with snook,
and toted 'round a debit book.

the guy to whom the boss would say
"you'll give this house two coats today".

whose menace was hamburger hash
when fifty cents was lots of cash

yes he's the one, your heart he'd steal
while harmonizing peg o'neal

but better days are here for him
his cup is full, up to the brim

there's no one i would rather see
have had that break, than i would, he

though fortune comes or even fame
he'll just be larry, just the same.

"war mothers" - 1942

mother's daily tasks are done
so - very tired she quickly sleeps,
relieved 'til dawn from work and care
from children's needs and house she keeps.
and while i see her gentle rest
as i begin to try to write,
i think of mothers cursed by war
who's sleep is robbed of them at night.

exhausted - but yet work to do
she must not sleep - but be alert
listen for the things that come
to cause her precious young some hurt.
she hears the pounding of her heart
and gentle falling of her tears -
pleasant sounds to little voices
terror-stricken, screaming fears.

sailor or soldier
(march 24, 1943)

behind them fades the friendly shore
before them lies the sea
beneath them lurks the deadly sub
they face eternity

no one says he is afraid
but stands beside his gun
and there he'll stay day after day
to see the voyage done

for he is the lifeblood of the men
that waits across the seas
together they take up the task
of freeing you and me.

listening

is it difficult to listen
to the stories often told
by people who have lived their lives
and now are getting old

minute details of incidents
stretch the stories out
you must appear concerned, sincere -
to learn what it's about

the antiquity may bore you
and events seem quite remote
and you tend to smile a little
as you listen to the quote

but <u>do</u> be kind and sacrifice
the minutes that it takes
for some day you'll be telling tales
of wisdom - and mistakes

one thousand strong

the Houston was a mighty ship,
she sailed the ocean blue,
she fought the battle to the end
each man was strong and true.

her crew is gone and she's at rest
beneath a troubled sea,
we pledge ourselves to right that wrong
and make the oceans free.

we, from Houston, heed her call
to see the battles done,
we will not rest or give an inch
'til victory is won.

though there be sweat, and blood, and tears
one thousand strong, we say,
the Houston did not sink in vain,
the Houston's here to stay.

no news - is -

when first i heard
of slings and arrows
i was very young
i did not cringe
at news of violence
when some poor soul got hung
i just read the comic page
and maybe baseball scores
i was running, swimming, laughing
some work, and household chores
but life was great and full of fun
not trouble, tears and pain
some newsfolks never see the good
they only see the stain!

give me time

there is no way i can return
to days that slipped away
i really do not want the things
i dreamed of yesterday

i wanted things that fit the times
for then i had the need
but things have changed as have the years
and likewise has my creed

each day is now more precious
in itself -it is a gift
time is what's desirable
it passes by so swift

just sometimes

sometimes the winding road steepens
sometimes the going gets rough
what used to be easy sailing
gets tiresome dreary and tough
new people new faces to choose from
the others "my friends" are all gone
i grope in new and strange places
being pushed around like a pawn
the uncertainty that each day brings me
is a challenge and yet it is true
just one day i'd like to be lonesome
and maybe a little bored too

nodding

all the time you're talking
you get my mind to thinking
and my head is nodding yes
and sometimes no -

this does not mean agreeing
all these nods that you are seeing
it's what you are expecting
me to show -

but i'm paying close attention
to everything you mention
i agree with very little
that you say

'cause the world is full of chatter
that really doesn't matter
and my nodding makes you happy
in some way.

the enemy

you have to study the enemy
if you want to win the war
you must understand the strategy
that's been employed so far
there are cunning ways to trap you
tho' all may look sincere
are your counterspies efficient
and alert to things they hear?
are your forces trim and ready
do they know what they must do?
you have to know your enemy
'cause the enemy is you.

that's the truth

the rest of your days
depend on the rest of your nights
fatigue can get you down
instead of being ring master
you'll end up being a clown
with tears in your eyes
and despair on your face
and shoes that don't fit your feet
sure you will make people laugh
but you'll have a big patch on your seat

we like to think

we like to think that the world is fine
and a wonderful place to be,
we think it is when we shun the things
we do not care to see.

we like to think that all men care
about their fellow man,
we force ourselves to think it so
as far as we really can.

we like to think there is happiness
spread wide and far to all,
but we know there's lots who just pretend
their number would appall.

so we ride along in a mythical dream
pretending ourselves as we go,
wishing with all the force we have
that life was really so!

looking on

the army of the unemployed
look all alike to me
they are all a bit self-conscious
as well as i can see

maybe they are scared to death
that they will get a job
although they look ambitious
while standing in the mob

to get smart

i sit and ponder
and often wonder
why i don't know more

these things are free
it's up to me
to tap the endless store

wreckage

the storm is past
and as we see
the gentle rolling
of the sea

and turn to view
the damage wrought
we learn a lesson
it has taught

slander not unlike
a storm
wheels a mighty
crushing arm

if you see it
rise to strike
cushion the blow
to those you like

whatever

sure the world is hectic
and things go wrong at times
but most of it is pretty fair
except for pain and crimes
the sun-the wind-the growing things
the tender glance-the love
all that live beneath the ground
and all that live above
combine to be the place we live
for better or for worse
it's yours to have just either way
to like or hate and curse

comfort

i'm gonna work my fingers to the bone
to get my house all bright
i want it snug and cozy
with the temperature just right
i want everything to please me
where i'll be safe at night
when i have it all fixed up
with locks that one can't break
i'll take my boat and camper
and head out to some lake
i'll sweat and burn and drink too much
and step upon a snake

busy busy

most everything we do's been done
if not in fact-in theory
except of course the cancer cure
and things as bad and dreary
but things like fly-and dive-and speed
mixed notes and colors pretty
there's lights for night cool air and warm
clear land and mighty city
we've fought and won and fought and lost
we've built and torn down
we've lived through tribe and kingdom
through president and crown
we changed our money back and forth
to now the "mighty" dollar
we've tamed the jungle-caged the beast
and led him on a collar
what next is there to do you ask
why we have just begun
we've yet to find tranquillity
that lets us live as "one"

temptation

taste of the thrill
but not too deep
too much will put
your soul asleep
and the drastic change
when you awake
will leave a mark
of some mistake
sip for the taste
and throb of heart
but do not rent
the thing apart
cherish the moments
left unscathed
exiting-yet
near well behaved

dear friend

when describing a friend
you seek words of praise
like loyal, thoughtful, and dear

like truthful and kind and helpful
nice and also sincere

you are my friend and i like you
i describe you with words
you see here

41

watch it!

the world
is out to
get you
but you
can turn
the tide
check before
you take
the road
on which
you'll fall
or slide
there're signs
hung up and down
the path to
help you on
your way
that tell you
where to walk
and watch
also what
to say
you'll never
have things perfect
but you can
darn well try
let things
that help
and teach you
go in your
ear and eye

whoa ! ! !

things done in haste
soon lead to waste
and funds and time
are lost
investigate
seek out and wait
set straight the need
and cost
another day
may bring a way
much better
than the first
you need not lose
if you can choose
'course one
may be the worst

blemish and stigma hurt

blemish and stigma hurt
repentance is painful too
but this is the penalty we must pay
for things we should not do
think twice before you do the thing
make sure you are equipped
to stand the pain and anguish
and the lashing of the whip

you are you alone

aspire at being a real good you
let the talents you have come shining through
    no matter how small they appear to be
    each has a gift that sets them free
we are not all alike-each persons's his own-
we are different-with things that are ours-alone
    it's amazing how well we all get along
    when you think of the thoughts in the minds of the throng
we are the specks on the crust of the earth
but you can be you for all that it's worth

you made you

it takes years to be a stinker
the repeater kind i mean
it takes years to be a nice guy
this of course is plainly seen
it takes practice to be perfect
so what you are today
is not coincidental
you arranged it all that way

the hard way

it's awfully hard to give youth
that beautiful asset in time
but it must be spent on the hard road up
it's a steep and awesome climb
it drains and fills your body
and your intellect
you die and learn a bit each day
and lose as you collect
soon you're smart and helpless
'cause you wore out getting smart
your brain's a mighty storehouse
and your body's near apart
this combination seems unreal
and should be turned around
but youth will learn the hard way
'til a better way is found

i must be calm

convention restricts me to quietly weigh the gruesome facts of life's multitudinous complexities

when i am completely and thoroughly exhausted with no solution in sight i must again conventionally and quietly utter pleading prayers and hope patiently for answers which my inadequate human nature is capable of devising

although i know better--god seems so far away i would like to stand on a high hill and in a loud high voice strained beyond capacity scream out in uncontrolled emotion

i also know that my problems are infinitesimal compared to most-especially those of a dying saviour-but witnesses at the foot of the cross relate that he cried out in a loud voice-"father, why have you forsaken me?"

"what a man"

no matter "what a man" you are,
or how she likes your face;
just remember there's another man
can always take <u>your</u> place.

don't think because <u>you</u> left her
that she's going to sit and cry;
she'll find another "what a man",
as they go marching by.

if you'd like to see her later,
or you'd like to have a date;
you had better start out early,
even then you may be late.

and if you are refused by her
and feel the sting of shame;
buckle up because you know she's right,
and you have just <u>yourself</u> to blame.

no matter

no matter how long you live
or if travels were near or far
no matter what you have done
or how smart you really are
no matter what pain you have suffered
or what sorrow you have known
no matter how crowded your life
or how long you have been alone
no matter how poor your existence
or how rich you are in cash
no matter how friends may accept you
or how with all others you clash
no matter your knowledge of things that were
or how well you stored them away
there's going to be another surprise
with almost every day

tears

you cry with the eye
and the reason why
is to let your emotions
express

there's no reason for shame
and no one's to blame
there's lots of things
tears can bless

tempest

there must be words
to amply describe
the frightening passing of time

there's no logical way to
express this truth
it has no reason or rhyme

there's a helplessness that
one often feels
as days slip quickly by

and you double up on the
things you do but time goes-
though stop it you try

seems yesterday was
awfully short
as likewise was today

tomorrow's sure to pass
as quickly
there is no other way

the horizon once so far
so far
comes plainly into view

it makes one
cherish passing time
as days are born anew

seesaw love

first you're up; then you're down;
now you laugh; now you frown;
now you give a sweet caress;
now you could not love me less.
now you're happy; now you're sad;
then you're gay; then you're mad.
all this being in suspense,
really does not make good sense.
you will never be content
'til your energy's well spent.
kill your grievance at the start,
you'll find it easy on your heart.
corrective criticism's good,
if you take it as you should.
i listen when you're finding fault,
and take it with a grain of salt.
when i suggest that something's wrong,
you protest loud and protest long.
i try to pass the matter off,
but all you do is fret and scoff,
until i want to pull my hair,
and fling it all in grim despair.
then i find i've lost my head,
and can't remember what i've said.
never once in four years long
have you admitted you were wrong,
but i love you just the same -
no matter who may be to blame.

don't do it

long is the way from the bottom up
vacant the taste from the empty cup
hard is the lash from the wagging tongue
flat is the echo from the song once sung
deep is the pit when the sun comes high
lost is the answer to why-oh why

leap year

it's february--'48
beware you unwed men
your earnings and your bachelorhood
are jeopardized again

it's time for caution, be on guard
for cupids aim is true
you're at a disadvantage
when the question's put to you

but don't feel bad if you succumb
don't blame it on the year
there's lots of us that thought we asked
but now it's all quite clear

extraordinary

if you'd like to have your trip through life
to be a pleasant tour
face up to things that vex you
and all you must endure
say yes when no is better
though the price is high
cut fight to fuss or nothing
hold back tears-don't cry
lash out at nothing-but yourself
and hold yourself in tow
be soft and kind and gentle
love everyone you know
if you do this and do it well
you never will be cursed
not only that you dummy
but you'll also be the first

i did it

someday i will be sitting
rocking to and fro
with nothing that i have to do
and no place i have to go
i will not hurry, fret, or fuss
nor answer ringing phones
i'll hardly have to move at all
just rest my weary bones
i'll think about those trying times
and with pleasure will recall
the fact i had it all to do
and that i did it all

i'm tired

they say my brain
is slightly used
its lack of work
is much abused
that i could learn much faster

what i know now
has made me tired
i need some rest
from what's required
much more would be disaster

the wonder of it all

the irish have a saying
"oh! the wonder of it all"
that covers time forever
from the rise until the fall
all that people have been doing
'til this very day
reaching out ahead of time
to find a better way
we make mistakes we've always made
we never seem to learn
tho - "the wonder of it all" is here
most everywhere you turn.

ordeal

i don't come in 'til after nine
i leave at four and that is fine
you come at eight and leave near five
that keeps the business well - alive
the telephone rings all day long
sometimes i hear you hum a song
i know not where you get the strength
technicalities never stop
paper fills our neat workshop
everything is filed away
on and on day after day
they call it business, not just work
a thing we do and must not shirk
i'm sure God knows what he's about
but he could have left this work thing out.

we'll have a steak

people born and bred

in Texas

never seem to get

their fill

of their favorite

food they cook

when they have

an outdoor grill

you should have

a charcoal burner

here's the money

it will take

go and buy one

and enjoy it

when we come

we'll have

a steak

march

the swirling twisting winds of march
blow loose the winter cloak
reminds the world there're other things
besides bare trees and smoke

there must be force to blast us free
of sitting near the fire
to end our hibernation too
and germinate desire

march seems the way to plant and grow
in woods throughout the land
it's nature's way of leading us
we hardly feel her hand

quote

"leave me alone for a minute
i have to relax or i'll die"
has been heard over and over
it's a universal cry
everyone must yield to pressure
retreat from it all-when one can
for stress will crumble and hurt you
it's a deadly destroyer of man
they can set your bones and sew up your cuts
and operate here and there
but tranquillity will only prosper
when you cut down on wear and tear

if you can

to understand the total whole
you must understand the parts
not just that something happens
but how it stops and starts
so when you see the symptoms
approaching on the scene
you'll recognize their purpose
and what they really mean
they predict the joy or sorrow
as they fit into a plan
so be on guard in choosing
especially-if you can

right or wrong

there's pros and cons on everything
that folks must talk about
and there is what is known as
the benefit of doubt

it's kind to let the other fellow
think that he is right
at least until you check around
and dig the answer out

then even if you find he's wrong
weigh carefully the prize
to prove that right was wrong -
could be poor judgement in disguise!

people tell me

if you're talking to me
i pay strict attention
i hear what you say
and details you mention
if your story is sad
i may get sad too
for most of the time
that's all i can do
i can't solve many problems
though i wish that i could
but when people tell me
i listen real good
if that helps them i'm grateful
because it is true
if folks would just listen
that's all they need do

silver spoon

you may have been born
with a silver spoon

but you still have to
pay the price

for effort rewards
with achievement -

not with the roll of the dice

compared to some

we are blessed with a bathroom small
with no big fish bowl in the wall
no polar bear rug upon the floor
an old-fashioned bolt locks the door
the ceiling's flat and near our heads
there's no chaise lounge or other beds
the mirror shows us slightly waved
often from memory have we shaved
the wash stand's small but it will do
it often serves in washing two
no mirrors make you a quartet
your prima donna while all wet
no special room to house your robe
we hang ours on the 'lectric globe
a meal for twelve a crowd would be
but we could handle four for tea
our toothbrush does not hang in class
we have to fish them from a glass
if your bathroom is like grant's tomb
come up and see a real bathroom
it may not satisfy the greeks-
but we come out with rosy cheeks

banish fear

lay hold the task and see it done
tho it takes days or years
then gather in the laurels won
and think back on your fears

those obstacles that loomed so high
are difficult to find
they were not real you passed them by
for they were in your mind

i reminisce

the echo of the tolling bells
shut tight one door of life
one blissful happy chapter with
one striking blow of strife

tomorrow came-the sun arose
a threshold loomed in view
at first 'twas hard then time slipped by
and there was much to do

the striking blow has waned away
there's naught but thoughts of bliss
birthdays bring it rushing back
for then i reminisce

little things

all the things you do for me
are held in high esteem
and everything is big to me
though little it may seem
you're full of nice surprises
and i thrive on joy they bring
each thing is just gigantic
'cause "there are no little things"

little things II

great paintings are done
by strokes of a brush
statues are sculptured
by chips and light touch
buildings are built
with brick upon brick
on a thin bed of mortar
to see that they stick
sand dunes are piles
of small grains of sand
pick up the earth
it is dust in your hand
be cautious of small things
for when they're arranged
they make up the big things
not easily changed

today

i got a good dose of emotion today
some was like blue skies, some was quite gray
i witnessed some things that should not have occurred
an undignified use of the spoken word
there was some soft language
with love in it's tone
nods of approval
which thrills to the bone
as the clock ticked on
and time slipped away
t'was more good than bad
like most every day

woman is blessed with emotions

woman is blessed with emotions
built with beauty and grace
tresses of hair to adorn her
and frame her pretty face
with power to sway events of the world
and mould the ways of man
to get him to do most anything
tho' he can't she tells him he can
so he does the thing, becomes the champ
and gathers in the prize
she smiles and thinks how easily
with help a man will rise

your boy

inside your lad is a smoldering flame
that can burst into being and lead him to fame
be gentle and firm to the right degree
you are molding a man who might someday be
a doer a thinker of some renown
entitled to wear the victor's crown
he may puzzle you now as you view with alarm
his turbulent life like a raging storm
be gentle and firm to the right degree
he has high potential-just wait you'll see

school's out

commencement means
beginning - but they
put it at the end
they tell you what
it's like out there
on this you must depend
"nothing's good that's easy"
"leave it better than you found"
"lots of things need changing"
"try to turn such things around"
"perfect your skills"
"go fearless forth"
"work hard at what you do"
you knew all this already
but now it all comes true.

hard to do

they talk about things
that are hard to make
like lenses and crystal
easy to break

towers of steel
that reach to the sky
a rocket that probes
since they taught it to fly

balloons full of water
on which you can sleep
a digital thing
that will count your sheep

a clock with no wheels
and no hands on its face
a weapon that shoots
some stuff they call mace

cameras that stop
the hummingbird's wings
dolls that can tinkle
and a robot that sings

but the human mind
will all it possesses
can't make up its mind
to solve its own messes

it'll be o.k.

i stand in the midst
of a mixed-up world
and i'm mixed up myself you know

i don't understand all
the things i see
as i ride with the ebb and flow

values change from day to day
what was right
is now all wrong

the tempo-the beat
the man in the street
sing out a wordless song

the right and the truth
and care-and love
fight for a place upstage

and they'll win you know
'cause they always do
history tells it on every page

procrastination

procrastination steals our days
and time goes by unused

ambitions gather tons of dust
and chances are abused

a good idea unless progressed
will tarnish-wane and fade

and leave an empty space in time
where failures all are made

the greatest loss

if you lose your home and money
something else will take its place
if you lose your job or business
or take last place in the race
if you have to sleep out in the park
or go around in rags
and like all of us you suffer
when the money value sags
all of this can be redone
repaired replaced forgot
you may wind up with little
and with little have a lot
but if somebody breaks your heart
and causes you despair
everything just disappears
and there is nothing anywhere

just be you

i'm tired of pretending
i'm somebody else
i think i'm just gonna be me
i'll try it a while
and check the results
and see how much
change it will be
if i've done it too long
that i'm too far gone
i'll stay as i am and i doubt
that folks will even detect at all
just what it is i'm about
'cause you see no one paid much attention
all the time i was acting the part
i could have been me for all of that time
and not kidded myself from the start

small sins

oh what a world
it could have been
without the burden
that we call sin
now i don't want
to start a war
just looking at things
the way they are
like the little sins
that eat away
always present every day
the energy that goes to waste
with words and jesters
poorly placed
we all pay dearly
for our faults
and lose the pleasures
small sins halt -

you too?

there are thousands of things
i'll never get done
they are very important
i must do each one

i sit and do nothing
and think of that stuff
not to sit and do nothing
gets pretty rough

so i do a few things
to meet life's demands
i sweat a lot
and scuff up my hands

but it's all done with pleasure
and sharpens my skills
some call it work
and that pays the bills

if i run out of things
that i just have to do
i'll be probably - sad
and near the end too!

start now

you know right now what is wrong with you
make a list if you have to
or just pick one thing that needs correction
and point yourself in that direction
slowly turn it all around
and make yourself behave
so now you have lost the fault
now what else do you crave?

i don't know how to do nothing

i don't know how to do nothing
i cannot just stare into space
i've been busy since i was a baby
life is a challenge - a race
i know i can not win the battle
i know i will lose in the end
but the challenge is fruitful and thrilling
the encounter with foe and friend
it's never a drag - i won't let it be
i'm nosie i guess in my quest
i like the fatigue from the battle
and the fun that i get when i rest
life is immense, it's gigantic
full of wonders, intrigue, and love
the good lord knows what he's doing
as he deals it out from above

sorrow's battle

there is no place to seek the peace
my soul keeps longing for
it can't be found in silence
or in crowded seminar

the lilting tones of sweet refrains
soothe not the burdened brow
bring tears a little quicker
presses down on one somehow

i'm embarrassed some at laughter
and pity those who mourn-
but i must fight off this sorrow
be ungrudging-not forlorn

so i'll laugh a little now and then
and listen to a tune
'cause i can't be sad forever
so i'd better end it soon

that's me

i'm prone to blame others for causing
the things that happen to me
but i wink at myself in the mirror
for there it is plain to see
that the fellow that causes me trouble
is making a dunce out of me

experience

experience is the best teacher
that isn't fiction it's fact
each day you advance in wisdom
as you watch and think and act

if your life isn't getting some better
as you go along day by day
it might help to change your system
and live life some other way

uncle ot

i used to be as strong as a bull
could swing an ax all day
i could plow with a horse and needed less rest
that to me was like play
i could work all day in a hundred and ten
or do chores to my waist in snow
i could walk to town and back again
and see as far as a crow
nothing was hard or tough to do
it was easy with muscle and brawn
i went to bed when the sun went down
and was up at the crack of dawn
it took a long time for me to run down
i can't do a lot anymore
i guess i've used up all my steam
of course i'm ninety-four

do it

the task is here
the time is now
you can do it
you know how
take some action
do one thing
some reaction
this will bring
take a step
a little nearer
you will see
the answer's clearer
fashion something
from your finding
see it through
make it binding
finalize with
closing touch
there-it's done
'twasn't much

the inhuman race

there's no time to sit
by the babbling brook
or walk in the meadow today
i've a million things
that just must be done
and the time is slipping away
I said the same thing yesterday
and the day before that i'm sure
it's always been a constant race
and this malady needs a cure
but the cure will have to wait a bit
'til I get all this other stuff done
i tell you the whole thing's crazy
it's a battle that can't be won

victim

i am a victim of everyday life
i absorb its pleasures and abhor its strife
i shudder at losses and cheer with each gain
i wear out my body and fill up my brain
i'm afraid and i'm brave depending you know
on the size of the thing
and the way that things go

all in the dictionary

i have a big dictionary here
it's full of magnificent words
if properly used in sequence
they tell of the bees and the birds
rearrange them and shift them about a bit
they'll tell what to do and do not
if you want to remember a lot of things
write them down and they're never forgot
you can use them to pray or to swear
it makes no difference you see
words are no good unless properly placed
there's a bunch misused seems to me
but we all like to talk and tell our views
and blab to our heart's content
and a lot gets said that's very good
but a lot gets said that ain't meant

each day

each day i'm put to the test
of one kind or another
each day i must dig out
or i will surely smother
each day the whole thing changes
so i bend to find my way
each day i must be valiant
and wait to meet
"each day"
but i'm not geared for trouble
so i falter and i fall
i'm better in tranquillity
but then are not we all

get away

to get away is the better way
to see a thing real clear
when you view it over day by day
you really are too near
so get away and then reflect
and segregate the facts
think clearly-put all things in place
when you are most relaxed
soon the answer will emerge
with reasons crystal clear
then of course you'll implement
with far less chance or fear

yesterdays

when tomorrows
become yesterdays
o'r and o'r again
and the things that
happened yesterdays
are harder to regain
when some memories of old
come cheerfully to mind
when a day that matches yesterday
is mighty hard to find
the richness that is living
comes in focus
bright and clear
each day you pull in closer
all the things that you
hold dear

to keep your soul and body clean

to keep your soul and body clean
pray, eat, wash, and move
pray to heaven, God, and saints
they understand your mood

eat fish and foul and things not sweet
eat greens and fruit galore
scrub with soap and water
chase dirt from every pore

exercise 'til sweat appears
and muscles are quite sore
try not to think of self and wants
think more of other's needs

give way to things that melt your heart
seek not a heart that bleeds
all this will make you happy
fulfill your heart's desire.

whitten's quitten

on the 4th of july
i'll know how it felt
to get up and say i'm free
'cause the 1st of july
in "90" it's going to
happen to me
i do not say i hated work
or going to and from
or taking care of money and adding
up the sum
i liked the folks i worked with
they are friends
i leave behind
it's been a great experience
but it's time
that i unwind

just watch

the frown, the smile, the eyebrow
the direction of the stare
the way the eyelids open
and others signs are there
your face can change the circumstance
and not a word be said
is that what folks are saying
when they stand head to head
i guess what folks are doing
is talking head to head

all alone

if i was alone in a wilderness
with the birds and bees
and such

i don't think i'd miss the things
i've learned to love
so very much

chances are i'll ner' be alone
except in my own
habitat

and believe me i don't look
forward to
a horrible fate like that

once or twice in my
little span
i have tasted such a fate

and i'd hate to face
another day
without my loving mate---!

i can't

when pain blocks out
all other thought
when you've lost the fight
you bravely fought
when the storm is holding
you at bay
when you should be out
and on your way
when very sad and
out of sorts
when conversation
brings retorts
when all's been bad
for quite a while
someone says
"come on now smile"
think of walking
on the beach
with your loved one
in your reach
when days were bright
and skies were blue
when laughter filled
you through and through
advice is great
and i will try
it's hard to smile
i'd rather cry

we differ

here teeming on the surface of
this thing called mother earth
there are countless human beings
each striving for his birth

no two desire the selfsame things
no two see eye to eye
no matter if they share a crust
or have no worldly tie

the nearest to utopia
that man will ever rate
will be when au have minimized
their differences and hate

speech

of all the gifts
that God bestows
the best one is
that of speech
it brings near the
attributes or pain
and keeps them
near in reach
it is a sound that
penetrates
the heart to
comfort, soothe, and
mend
and radiates pure
love or pain with
the message that it sends

and the winner is -

i say to myself
says me to i
does it help me live
or make me die
i want to live
and stretch my span
to be a well and happy man
so i'll think and do
what will stretch the days
so they will win the game life
plays

worry

a prudent human decision
is the best I can hope to attain
when there hangs in the balance something
which will cause me to lose or gain

some say that I worry with gusto
they detect from behavior somehow
it's my preoccupation or frowning
so easy to see on my brow

but i'm giving due vent to the problems
so i'll have an answer that's good
it's a prudent human decision
call it worry if you should

it is done

i will not move from here
not tomorrow nor for a million years
the things i have done are done
many i could have done better
many i should not have done at all
many i left undone-in fear neglect or foolishness
i loved many things-the odors the touch the sights the sounds
i loved many people-each in a different way
each to a different degree
i tried to hate nothing or no one
i am sorry for my offenses to all
particularly to my redeeming savior

85

"tick"

clocks the world over
tick away seconds
those remaining can hold
unexcelled exhilaration
what a dreadful waste
if one second was neglected

"tock"

concentrate

the name of the game is concentrate
'cause what you think you do
control your head and stay ahead
you'll be a lot smarter too
the brain is your nearly perfect tool
its ability knows no bounds
it gives power strength and knowledge
to the system which it crowns
your input makes it dull or sharp
it channels to where it is led
so concentrate on proper things
and have a good brain in your head

seems to me

out of each life there is something
that must be accomplished in time
not at the start or beginning
for then we are learning to climb
not in the teen or the fun years
when life is all love and sublime

but shortly thereafter the challenge
eagerly seems to appear
accomplishment must bc dealt with
the problem is now and here
we must be responsible adults
willing to act without fear

these are the years for the doing
it's now or never you know
for swiftly the busy time passes
it's desperate to watch as they go
you race to attain that great goal
with seeming little to show

then the mellow years drift in slowly
and the past is so easy to see
all those young dreams of the future
are here-or they were not to be
the thing that we did was the living
a joy in itself-seems to me

your fault

if i get into trouble you will be the one to blame
when we must meet an emergency you're the one that's lame

i get coordination from everyone but you
why is it that you say the things that i don't want you to

i have to make apologies for you most every day
it's all because you wag too quick in such an awful way

do you always have to step in just when things are looking bright
and on a happy situation throw a different light

or when we're in a jam why can't you be still
there's something that's not up to par that you just have
to spill

i try to keep you curbed and trained but it's so hard to do
you're not at all ambitious just what is wrong with you

As long as there's a spark of life and power in my lungs
i'll try to make you tongue of mine like educated tongues

you see

to me-i see-what i'm to be
what i'm to be i am
if you can see why so i be
that's all i give a damn

next

if all i do means nothing
and life is just a sham
i soon disintegrate to dust
they say that's all i am
in the few years that i spent here
all i did is soon forgot
i may have been successful
or let all go to pot
well at least my name was written
in that great big book of time
the world must have new people
it's your turn 'cause i've had mine

lull in love

it's not as if i don't recall
the things i used to say
it isn't that i did forget
our pleasant yesterday

but bills and kids have such a way
of coming in between
and i have to look ahead so far
it dwarfs the things i've seen

now one day when our job is done
and we rest back we two
i'll say the things i used to say
for then you'll know they're true

happy me

few people think of norman
'cause his birthday's in december
so he's kind of over-happy
'bout the people who remember
especially those who think in terms
of comfort sleep and rest
and of all the things i'm needing
pajamas are the best

yes

if i were to do it all over again
i'd do it about the same
i'd make a lot of dumb mistakes
and find someone else to blame
NO
i'd love much more and hate much less
i'd think much less of self
i'd take more knowledge from the books
not leave them on the shelf
i'd fashion a key to heaven's gate
and keep it tucked away
then i'd take my friends and loved ones
through the gate someday

give me a man

give me a man with a boiling point
who slowly lets it rise
who meets the dregs of sorrow
with tear-dimmed weary eyes
a man that chokes up easy
at sentimental bits
a man who likes to love and laugh
and never hollers quits

better fix it

the root of all evil
is not the buck
which by the way
is nice

it's true we must all
scratch for the coin
for everything
has a price

nothing is free
not even fresh air
it takes millions
to clean it for use

our war on nature
is awesome
it must come
to a reasonable truce

don't blame all trouble
on money
it's people that cause
the most pain

we'd better get with it
and fix it
i hate to drink
acid rain

papa test

chin up old boy when baby cries
and keeps you up all night
you'll smoke a thousand cigarettes
and pray the morning's light

that tender voice that coos so cute
can raise an awful stink
at three or four or five o'clock
till you can hardly think

you have to go to work next day
while mom and baby rest
to see if you can stand some more
and pass the papa test

do it for

don't spoon out the things
you do each day
seeking praise-returns or reward
lamenting that folks don't notice
that you are trying so hard

take pleasure from just
the simple fact
that you did what you did
out of love
the greatest reward is internal
all else is below-not above

i wish

lots of things
start with
a wish
and a lot
of wishes
come true
the wish is really
the thing that
it takes
to make you do
what you do
you can wish
your whole
life through
and never
accomplish a thing
or get up and do
what you have to
and have the things
it will bring

"keep out"

if you want to survive
keep a "keep out" sign
always in your mind's view

cautiously think and
guard what you say - don't rush
to strife - made by you

you are dealing
with folks exposed to life
just as all other's do

they don't feel
a whole lot better or worse
oh, of course there may be a few

but hurt is hurt and
love is love and
it's often all up to you

what a day

there are times
when life gets awful

things go from
worse to bad

days are full
of nothing

except what's
bleak or sad

rainbows do not
grace the skies

nothing seems
like play

hurry up tomorrow
and be a different day

of course i will

will you be watching me
of course i will
will you help me in temptation
of course i will
will you comfort me in sorrow
of course i will
will you help me to learn of you
of course i will
will you teach me to pray
of course i will
will you be my best friend
of course i will
will you be here forever
of course i will
will i see you someday
of course you will

slow down

i can not see for the life of me
why i must rush and hurried be

i've been north and south and saw each sea
life's been mighty good to me

i have a storehouse full of things
i don't need much that money brings

i just need love from those who care
and escape from mental wear and tear!

it's painful

it's painful to love
it's painful to hurt
it's painful to give
it's painful to flirt
it's painful to spend
it's painful to save
it's painful to hide
it's painful to crave
it's painful to find
it's painful to seek
it's painful to know
it's painful to peek
it's painful to laugh
it's painful to cry
it's painful to live
it's painful to die

lost and found

what joy it brings
to have it in your clutch
you thought that it was gone
that thing you loved so much
if it is a person
your pain is multiplied
you long to have them standing
right there by your side
the worst thing really happens
and that's the highest cost
reverse the lost and found
and you'll get found and lost

this day

who is to say
when the day is done
if the effort spent
has lost or won
everyday we win or lose
by the things we say
and the thoughts we choose
the reckless tongue
and the untamed mind
outweighs the god
and we drop behind!
learn this day and save tomorrow
have more fun
and lots less sorrow.

to lose control

to lose control and be a slave
to a habit that wrecks your life
is to paint the way to pain and loss
a constant road of strife

the now renewed at each sunrise
see failure as it sets
and one more day is wasted
steeped in more regret

the hopeless anguish prays the mind
and kills off each day's joys
leaves a wretched human
lacking judgement, sense, and poise

one of life's great victories
is concerning such a plight
and being rid of misery
that killed life's great delight

the dawn of love

the first five years
are the hardest
one fifth of that
is gone
we have past
the test of nearness
in our love affair
of dawn
so we enter
into loving
for a period
of time
eternal-true
and thrilling
forever
and sublime

heart of gold

the warmth of love
embedded here
within my heart of gold
is not revealed
by what i do
for i am prone to scold
the sting of tongue
the sudden glance
the unsaid word
is bad
my heart of gold
is tarnished black
and all my world
is sad

impending doom

disaster lurks at every turn
no matter what you do
but if you think of this alone
your life will soon be through
some bad thing's going to get you
the one you least suspect
so why not look to pleasant things
until your life is wrecked
if it's going to happen anyway
be gay until the crash
at least you'll have some memories
to help distract the smash

hidden talents

bottled up inside of you
are talents by the score
you'll learn this is a fact and true
if only you'll explore

don't say - oh - i can not do that
'cause you can do that - and more
so try a few unusual things
you've never done before

a whole new world may open up
and thrill you to the core

hug me

a hug is worth
a thousand words
and you are
out of reach
you can not hear
"i love you"
you can not
hear my speech
i should be standing
next to you
doing what i miss
and never be
no farther than
each can throw a kiss

"He" said

brush off the dust
from the trip just done
the old routine
has it's trophies won
away up ahead
is a brand new goal
with things to do
that will flood your soul
i hear the heavens
sing your praise
as prayers and works
fill all your days

that's me

i cannot be like anyone else
i must follow my star
i follow each path in life as it comes
it worked out fine so far
when i hurt, i hurt to the core
when i'm sad, i'm as sad as can be
when i'm happy, i show it with force
that everyone can see
what you see is what i am
very easy to read
if you need someone with practice
i'm the guy you need

please

the arms of God
are open wide
there's room for all
within
it's just a short trip
all can take
but first you must
begin
so set a goal
a short way off
to feel this great
embrace
your body, soul and
everything
will fill with joy
and grace

to give

to give is ---
> just to give
with neither string
> nor weight
to give is ---
> just to give
not manipulate

the giver who ---
> forgets the gift
is blessed ---
> a hundred-fold
that gift ---
> is treasured
most of all ---
> a privilege
to behold

real sorrow

from every pore
your sorrow bleeds
your heart is drained
of joy
all pleasant things
look back at you
like some - now
broken toy
the long way back
is hard and sad
it makes the strong
seem weak
nothing seems
to fill the gap
now empty dark
and bleak
days run by or linger
tears still come
and go
your sorrow is the same
but does not seem
to show
nice things
blot out sad things
leaving threads of hope
that maybe down the road
some day you'll get the strength
to cope

conquest

when backed against a wall of fear
there seems to raise from somewhere near
the strength to fight and overcome
lest we give up and so succumb
this reservoir cannot be tapped
until all other help is sapped
companion to this strength so great
is understanding of your fate
somehow you know the end result
a kind of ecstasy is felt
your strength and knowing spur you on
soon your problem is all gone
though bruised and beat and oft dismayed
another conquest has been made

christmas eve 1965

it's strange that i have time to write
although it's christmas eve
midnight mass is hours away
until we have to leave

time was when all the kids were small
we'd have so much to do
we'd rush and fret and pray
and barely get all through

we had the presents "hid" away
or stored in neighbors' rooms
there were pots and pans and dishes
things hard to wrap like brooms

there were bikes to be assembled
there were wagons, beds, and dolls
there were boxes full of lots of things
and animals with growls

there were packages of every size
paper, string, and glue
they was every color known
including mother's blue

so now the days are different
and the memories are sublime
"these different days" will turn to dreams
and fill another time

no comment

"no comment" means an awful lot
no matter where it's said
it means a lot of different things
and leaves a subject dead

it means that i may hurt myself
or that i may hurt you
it means i'd better hold my tongue
it's surely best i do

it means that what i'm thinking-
i'd better not reveal
it means that if i say it
you'll know just how i feel

i say it to confuse you
and make you wonder why
to never know the answer
no matter how you try

there's a way

there's a way
but i don't want to do it
'cause i don't want things to change
there's a way
but i'd have to start over
after the pains it took to arrange
there's a way
but i hate to venture
down avenues that are strange
there's a way
but the taste is bitter
and the pain is way out of range

careful

be sure that the source
of advice that you seek
is adequate to the task
it may be smart
to weigh it well
depending on whom you ask
not always does
the answer lie
in big successful tales
for some lessons are
much better learned
from one who tries and fails

life of a penny

i am a penny new and red
upon my front a stately head
a floral wreath adorns my back
but soon i will be old and black

my latin will be hard to read
to see my date a glass you'll need
poor abe will lose his face and hair
and i'll be thin from constant wear

but i'll still buy a candy stick
be good in some magician's trick
i'll make the gum machine turn loose
and make the scale your weight produce

i'll nestle in the best of bags
or jingle in the slits of rags
i hope i travel 'round a lot
hopping in and out of slot

i want to visit candy stands
tightly clutched in little hands
the thing i dread is that last plank
that lands me in a piggy bank

behold our flag

we stand here poised
to watch our flag
unfurling in the breeze
and dream the dream
of little girls
all satisfied and pleased

time was when men and
women dreamed-
dreams of deep despair
their only hope was in
this flag-
which we see flying there

we reap the harvest
of their hope
and bless the days
gone by
that gave us peace
and happiness
and keep our flag
on high

aircastles

when time's heavy on your hands
you can dream of other lands
other places far away
where you'd like to go someday
to the sunny shores of spain
or the rocky coast of maine
where the whitecaps bubbling break
on our greatest northern lake
to travel irish style
through the dear old emerald isle
to hear the jungle hum
mixed with black man's signal drum
on norwegian fjords to sail
'neath the mountain's purple veil
to scale the mighty wall
near an alpine waterfall
in the southland to repose
in spotless linen clothes
to gaze on desert sand
from a pyramid built by hand
to stand 'neath a london tower
as the bells toll out the hour
and to hear and see those things
that extensive travel brings

remember youth

remember youth as you grow old that once you were a boy
you kicked a-many tin can and broke a-many toy
you didn't wear your rubbers when you played up in the lot
you didn't do your homework and answered "i forgot"
you often went to parties and stayed as late as two
and didn't do one-half the things your ma had asked you to
if someday you raise a lad there's one thing that is sure
you're going to learn exactly what parents must endure

no good

if things are going from bad to worse
and you're failing to manage your task
don't go it alone-seek adequate help
then bury your pride and ask

it was never a sin to say i don't know
even if you know you should
the sin would be to wreck the thing
with a final result of "no good"

let's face it

everyone has many faces
everyone's changes with age
but other things change and shape them
like being thrown into a rage

smiles straightens out wrinkles
and pity makes muscles sag
inquisitive faces ask questions
i'm not sure why the eye has that bag

they say we make our own faces
and there's reasons that it is true
i guess it's the way we go along
and all of the things we go through

it's the one part of our body
that's hard to keep out of sight
so we must do more and more smiling
so our faces will look alright!

●

my 'lectric door

for years the door went up and down
several times a day
it strained my arms, my neck, and back
"i hate that door," i'd say

but all of that is in the past
no longer must i strain
i don't get sore, not anymore
nor wet in case of rain

my "thoughtful" husband noticed
and bought a 'lectric door
not even twelve red roses
would have pleased me more

gadgets

my life is full of lots of things
gadgets big and small
some i have and some i don't
some i don't need at all
but i am a "thing" man tried and true
to things i am a slave
why i have things i've never used
for time i never save

too bad

the distress the wars the daily strife
that plague the world and kill off life
are recorded in a million books
dusty now for no one looks
we all forget the rugged past
because today is-rushing-fast
there is no time for calm review
to see what now is best to do
so on man stumbles snatching crumbs
seeking pleasures-adding sums
the past could tell us-we could learn
but on we rush without concern
we travel on in dark deceit
grumbling at the fate we meet

see us through

to the army and the navy
to the coast guard and marines
we send this one request
"please see us through"

fire your rounds of ammunition
keep alive our great tradition
there is nothing that a free man
cannot do

the sun

i have mixed emotions about the sun
and how it measures time
i've watched it set and watched it rise
all were views sublime
the sunrise says "come on let's go"
the sunset says "let's rest"
but as it does it steals from me
the thing i treasure best
my life is measured out in days
this sun that comes and goes
depletes my time in segments
and what's left nobody knows

i pray

i pray while things are going well
when it's tranquil and sublime
'cause when i'm steeped in trouble
i really don't have time

but while i'm praying and at peace
i have it understood
that i'll get back to praying
when things are going good

mountain view

i came to see the countryside
my family and their dog
however i was hampered
by dark clouds and by smog

i rode in wooded mountains
and i swear i really tried
but my view was cut to just five feet
that is to either side

the mountains disappeared in clouds
the valleys filled with fog
so all i really got to see
was my family and their dog

reach down

no matter what station you hold in life
there is someone not doing as good
why don't you reach down with a helping hand
you'd feel so good inside if you would

fingernails

fingernails are pretty things
if you don't try to eat 'em
better leave those nails alone
'cause someday you might need 'em

of course you don't need fingernails
to play a violin
and when you use a typewriter
they're always buttin' in

but let a big mosquito nip you
on your leg or face
and i bet you'll wish your
fingernails were up there in their place

121

night storm

the lightning splatters patterns bright
across the darkened sky
the thunder pounds from sky to earth
it's louder with each try
but here beneath our little roof
with windows fastened tight
we feel secure from storm and rain
and do not fear the night
and there upon their little beds
our children asleep serene
they do not know the storm performs
with all its dreadful scenes
rage on oh storm
and spend thyself
then do be gone and stay
tomorrow they will wake to see
a fresh and brand new day

almost done

well we're just about done
with the job that we had
sometimes i'm sorry
sometimes i'm glad
there was spankin's and cryin'
much laughter and tears
there were scratches and fallin's
spread over the years
there was schooling and learning
piano and dance
there were questions galore
with a quick loving glance
there were meals in the morning
the evening and noon
there were prayers to be learned
and to carry a tune
there was washing and ironing
of ruffles and frills
hair by the miles
and drawers full of bills
it was sad here and there
but most of it fun
it's still just as happy
as when it begun
these are the things
that my memory brings
of course i left out
a book full of things

if

if you're feeling good
and you're clean and neat
and you're standing firmly
on two feet
if you love all men
and will forgive
if you're careful
with the life you live
if you spread good will
and are not curt
if you ask for pardon
when you hurt
you will not spend
a bad day one
and life will be
more joy and fun

pretty good

how many times have i wondered
as through life i plodded along
if what i was doing was the best i could
or was the whole thing maybe wrong

like most things it all turned out pretty good
in fact it was just right for me
it's a shame we can't see the future
and how pretty good it will be

kevin

the ball was thrown awfully bad
and after i gave it all i had
i missed the ball and it hit the fence
the stands were wild-the moment tense

i finally got the elusive ball
after a rather graceful fall
the runner was on his way to third
at about the speed of a hummingbird

i raised my arms as i always do
to make my throw-straight and true
i nailed the guy and he was out
the stands went wild-and did they shout

"hold it! hold it!" cried the ump
"he's safe" as he gave the "arms out" pump
the ump's decision broke my heart
as my beautiful world fell all apart

the other team soon won the game
and even if i was to blame
as long as baseballs keep on bouncin'
i'll love baseball-signed kevin johnson

all to all

since i do not fully comprehend
your attitude on things
it's difficult to navigate
and not disturb your mind

so i beg you to forgive me
when my action sorrow brings
it's hard to understand oneself
or why i was unkind

advice

there's gonna be a lot of times
when you will need advice
we'll be mighty happy
and think it rather nice

if with your trials and troubles
you'll come to mom or dad
we'll be most sympathetic
trust in us and you'll be glad

beginning to end

youth sits and stares
at each other
for hours and hours
on end

they walk in the woods
and giggle
they get along fine
without friends

look at the old folks
they whisper
why they just sit there
and rock

but the old folks have
lots of memories
one for each tick
of the clock

we hurt

who is the bad
or the good guy
it's hard to see
though you try
as events unfold
about you
there emerges a
reason why
but you do not
hear the reason
the sideshow
takes over the act
the main event's
in the background
and the sideshow
covers the fact
the overpoliteness
the quiet the tenseness
prevail too much
the answers to questions
are muffled
and dry are lips to touch
deep is the hurt
that's never expressed
an ending that could
have never been guessed

changes

things will not always
be pleasant
there'll be problems
along the way
just remember that
everything changes
it's always been
that way
try to be ready
and un-surprised
prepare as best
you can
treat the change
as a challenge
carefully watch
and plan
don't despair
keep you head in the air
maneuver always and pray
you will come out on top
be stronger and wise
it's always been
that way!

i forget

if i could talk to you tonight
and tell you how i feel
i'd open wide your childish eyes
and in your heart i'd steal

i'd tell you how i did not care
about your dirty hands
i'd tell you that i'm interested
in all your little plans

i'd play your games i'd read to you
i'd be the nicest dad
that any child alive
will get or ever had

the world has such a gruesome way
of making me forget
yet letting me remember some
enough to bring regret

do it

do it!
do it!!
do it!!!
don't just sit
and think
do it!
do it!!
do it!!!
don't sit on
the brink
do it!
do it!!
do it!!!
do it well
and good
do it!
do it!!
do it!!!
most people
could that would

?

i wonder what people are thinking
while they sit and stare into space
no one could tell what they're thinking
by the look that they have on their face

maybe it's finance they're checking
there's income expenses and needs
no matter how long they ponder
their expenses their income proceeds

maybe they must choose twixt something
a position investment or mate
their decision is based on the facts that they have
and the answer must not come too late

so when you see somebody dreaming
with a stare that is empty and long
don't try to guess what they're thinking
for percentages prove you'd be wrong

ask and receive

stop for a second
after you win -
how did i do this
how did it begin
did i get outside help
from others who know
the path i should tread
should i go fast or slow
will i win lose or draw
with the facts as they look
are rewards really worth
the chances i took
well here i stand
with the prize in my hand
so i thank god again
that i followed as planned

test yourself

test yourself and know your strength
pull every fiber taut
make note of pressures you can stand
in every battle fought

watch those who fall and topple
learn where they were short
be careful to examine what it did
to mind and heart

set tight your feet and live with force
frown not upon retreat
it's possible with caution
you may never taste defeat

you will know the warmth of life
and feel the glow of fear
but never dash yourself apart
when tragedy is near

i wait

i guess i should be reading books
to drink their knowledge in
consume the phrases one by one
to fight off deadly sin

but here in silence left alone
in quietness apart
i sense the nearness of my god
who'd like to have my heart

so tho' i understand the need
i think i'll silent be
and let him find me waiting
if he'd like to speak to me

"bob"

i am from up boston way
i'm a short and chubby guy
round about the middle
and my forehead's getting high

when i laugh i chuckle hard
my eyes just dance with glee
i laugh at folks in texas
and i guess they laugh at me

they "you all" that and "you all" this
and "yonder" "fetch" the thing
they "carry" folks from place to place
and my! the songs they sing
they "brag on things" and "fix to go"
they've "winner" when it's cold
everyone's a "good ole boy"
on texas they are sold

i must sound strange with "pardon"
and the way that i say car
there's no one who understands me
when i am saying "r"

i guess i'll stick to texas
with its bugs, its sun and rain
until i buy that little place
i dream about in maine
i think i still can make it
i have thirty years or more
or maybe i'll like texas best
when i am sixty-four!

back home

when i was just a little girl
i loved our house and town
i knew some day i'd leave it all
so my memory wrote things down
sure i went home now & then
things did not change so much
being gone is not the same
because you cannot touch
so here i am i'm back again
it's better than you think
to tell the truth "i love it"
like they say "i'm tickled pink"

easily found

if you are seeking happiness
you've got to think just right
be cheerful in appearance
and say things that delight
'cause the things that make for happiness
that you can have-or lack
are measured by what you give out
for that's what bounces back

137

yes it is

do nothing and stay out of trouble
do nothing and lose lots of sleep
do something to solve a problem
and another problem you'll keep
this thing about speaking up bravely
can shatter and rent apart
divide and tear asunder
and break a many heart
but to sit and be meek and say nothing
can rip the insides out of you
like the favorite words of all victims
it's hell if you don't or do

being human

i marvel at the human side
of everything well done
the preparation that it took
the bad mistakes made fun
the practice time uncounted
the exhaustion calling halt
the no one else to blame it on
and more obstacles to vault
the almost there-the do or die
the effort mustered up
the final thrust to victory
and then the loving cup

big difference

the coliseum's empty
i can hardly see my way
there's nothing going on here
but i think i'll sit and stay
i wonder where the clowns are
with their antics on the floor
where is the awful tiger
with his long teeth and his roar
i still can see the flyer
he was bouncing in the net
after doing all the reckless things
i never will forget
what's that-oh that's a hockey puck
and there's a basketball
there's tennis nets and running tracks
and folks dancing at the ball
i later went to see the place
and reminisce once more
but the building's gone forever
it is now - department store?

everything you mention

everything you mention
reminds me of my own
an experience or place or thing
(a sound) exact in tone
and as you switch
from place to thing
to person or to mood
i switch too, and nod my head
as if i understood
we all do that
it's nothing new
the reasons rather clear
there's hardly anything goes on
<u>that</u> <u>we</u> <u>don't</u> see or hear
i can think of lots of things
that don't come up too much
but we saw or heard it
if we're reasonably in touch

october 21, 1981

it was not here
that i chose to be
and, of course, i came
not to write
but i know not where
i would write the same
as i live here
day and night
no, i am not locked
in prison
soon i will be
"let go"
but confined i am -
i do as i'm told
and the process
is mighty slow
there is anguish and fear
the unknown is bleak -
i guess and surmise
about ills -
time is measured
from dawn to dusk
by needles, pressures and pills
those of us here
will be moving along
lucky to be on
our way
returned to health
and vigor
but the hospital staff
must stay.

excellence

if you are
opening a heart
or just cutting the grass
you must do
what you do
your best
and with class
not so the world
will proclaim you
are great
but so you will know
your very own fate
you can do well
and you can
feel great
just being you

don't tell

if you trip on yourself
and fall on your face
don't jump up and say i did it
dust yourself off
retreat if you can
you may not have to admit it

don't tell everyone
the mistakes you have made
it's better they stay under cover
it's bad enough we have to admit
to the ones that others discover

heaven help

when i lay me down to die
i know i'm gonna weep and cry
i'll try to wipe out yesterdays
and wish for time to mend my ways
but if alas it is too late
i hope a friend is at the gate
my heart was not in any sin
so maybe they will let me in

come on world

let's get better
at what we do
we can change it
if we change too
love thy neighbor
and all that stuff
even if it does
get rough
we know the rules
but we don't obey
i think that's all
i have to say

don't go too far

confidence is knowing
just how smart you are
and to hold your tongue
in tow
so you don't go too far
once you cross that point
the truth will then
stand out
and everyone will know
that your knowledge
just ran out!

africa

the earth is mostly water
and of course there's lots of land
right there under you -
right there where you stand

and there are lots of people
just like you and me -
standing somewhere else
that i'd really like to see

there's one place filled with animals
all free to roam the land
monkeys - zebras - lions - hippos
elephants! & apes with human hands

oh yes, the vulture and the snakes
they call this "home sweet home"
it's rich in gold and ores
africa has all of this -
that's where i'd like to roam

dear doctor

don't treat me as a thing of wood
or number on your file
i'm helping you to ply your trade
i'm sick once in a while

i trust in you and in your skills
i'm grateful you are there
to pick my pills and patch me up
i'm grateful when you care

i know that you get out of sorts
and you too hurt some days
so we're kinda like each other
in a lot of ways

i walk around with bones and blood
with veins and hair and teeth -
and lots of other parts, but still
i'm human underneath

define "great"

lost a great friend
the other day
went with him
a lot to say
we were friends
for many years
shared our joys
and sometimes tears
had a rather nice rapport
he never was cross
never a bore
played the game
with genteel force
always seemed
to be on course
took the bad
with poise and grace
was right at home
most any place
kept his secrets
tucked away
they're still with him
'til this day
he had traits
to emulate
makes friends like him
be just "great"

"bigger"

our child says she is bigger now
she says that she is three
inquisitive of things that are
and why they should so be
why do we have lights at night?
when does morning come?
what is ice cream made of?
and why can't she have some?
if clocks tick off the minutes
where do the minutes go?
when skies are dark and dreary
why does it not snow?
why is it she cannot smoke?
who put the foam on beer?
why don't we light the furnace
at this time of the year?
we face this inquisition
furnish answers as we go
when my bigger girl is bigger
think of all that she must know

nothing happens

i woke upon a sheet of white
a downy pillow held my head all night
the sun was screaming welcome as i arose
a carpet soft received my shoeless toes
a water faucet answered to my hand
a perfumed bar of soap was on its stand
a fluffy towel pat dry my waking skin
a song of some wild bird came softly in
i had to choose from many things to wear
i watched me-in a mirror-brush my hair
i primped a bit then lightly tripped the stairs
i don't remember having any cares
the folks all said "good morning" so did i
and i said nothing happens-wonder why

free advice

the best way to get it finished
is to start
initiate some action and be sure
you do it smart
of course you must have knowledge
do not tread outside your sphere
that will only cause you strife
and alter your career
so early in the ballgame
be sure you're on good ground
or someday just start over
when no one is around

friend

because of our fine friendship
and thinking as i do
how many happy memories
i have because of you
not just the thoughtful things you've done
but joys we've shared as well
that make our friendship memorable
and refreshing to re-tell

give & take

there is just so much
you'll have to do
to get from birth to grave
you will influence
more than you think
by what you give or crave
give as much as possible
for the other fellows' sake
and what you want
will come to you
there'll be little
you'll have to take!

"under the gun"

the only thing
under the gun
should be
the bottom of a drawer
lots of people
are under the gun
and are suffering
because they are
now "under the gun"
was coined to tell
that things are going bad
and no matter what you do
you always end up sad
but lift the stones
and scan the road
for sure you'll finally see
on every dark horizon
will be dawn
to set you free

too much trouble!

it's too much trouble for some folk
no matter what the chore
if it takes a little effort
they seem to hate it more
shadows even cast on fun
and pleasure turns to pain
and the lazy turn to brooding
and to lethargy again!

the winner is

the higher the hill
the harder to climb
the more to do
the shorter the time
the more to gain
the harder to choose
the freer the mind
the less it will lose
the prize that's won
the richer gets
the - time and pressure?
no regrets

that's what you said

yeah! that's what i said
and i'll say it again
not in the same place i hope
'cause the person that heard it
again and again
could wash out my mouth with soap
but the story's so good
and i tell it so much
that it grew to a beautiful lie
if it's heard just once
in the proper place
it gets better each time i try

testing

sometimes life takes awesome turns
and patterns start to form
peace of mind is shattered
and we view them with alarm
but this is only change at work
teaching us to cope
and to single out our path in life
paved with strife and hope
after all the smoke has cleared
that ravaged us with choice
we come out fairly well indeed
if we follow - inner voice

153

go - go - go

the clock is ticking
scramble - hurry
you won't get done
just work and worry
you can no longer
sit and stare
you must be sharp
alert, aware
these times demand
an interface
get in the swing
place in the race
prime your pump
keep it running
have the thing
for which you're gunning
don't give up
stand up and fight
exhaust yourself
with all your might

growing for us

plant life has certain durations
some short and some long - it is true
some furnish fragrance and beauty
charming our lives as they do
others cure pain tho quite ugly
others just bow with the breeze
some make our eyes itch and tearful
others of course make us sneeze
redwoods are almost forever
thousands of years so they say
while frail brilliant plants in the desert
struggle to last out a day
the rose is the first choice of many
a dozen red roses says "love"
but the olive branch brings the best message
when clutched in the feet of the dove

the shadow

why is there always a shadow
why this constant snag

why this uncomfortable feeling
that always seems to lag

it takes the smiles from faces
it changes the tone of voice

it alters desire and use
stifles the freedom of choice

i tire of innuendoes
and long for carefree days

i'll do anything to change it
there must be many ways

think good

the gift of life
is a precious gift

filled with joy and
love and care

the things that make
life hard to live

are the obstacles
here and there

to circumvent, to minimize
to challenge or attack

to muster up what
it will take

so peace of mind
comes back

the mental state
controls it all

tranquility will win

but only if the
mind obeys

and lets just good
things in!

157

the blues

don't ever write down
what causes your blues
'cause the blues
will come back if you do
time will erase
the trouble you had
released by something new
yesterdays gone
tomorrow's not here
today is of value to you
it excuses the past
and looks ahead
and both could
pull you through

daytime

time is now - it's time to do
not a time to fret and stew
the past is fine - the future bright
but now is now and time is right
so move and do the thing at hand
use every skill at your command
tho' it be work or just plain fun
do it well once you've begun
as life's moments fade and die
each has value if you try
don't let days just waste away
use them up - 'cause days don't stay!

it's people

i have watched this thing
for a long time now
more than 70 years in all
not as a casual observer
but for things i'd like to recall
it's people that really intrigue me
inexhaustible subject i know
but i've tried to study people
so i'd help me, and mine, to grow
things stand still 'til we move them
but people are changed by a glance
or inconsequential things
that start wars, pure fun, or romance
carefully pick your path through life
seeking, avoiding with care
'cause people are really your problem
not things - new, used, or rare!

hammers and nails

hammers and nails
and boards with knots
things that need fixing
like lawnmowers and cots
some things wear out
and just get old
some can't stand the wind or heat
and some just die
because of the cold
rocks wear away
leaving piles of sand
that can't be fixed by the human hand
lots of things are in the same fix
to these it's well to just say nix

that's me

i cannot be like anyone else
i must follow my star
i follow each path in life as it comes
it worked out fine so far

when i hurt i hurt to the core
when i'm sad i'm as sad as can be
when i'm happy i show it with
all my force that everyone can see

that's us?

we may well be hurting ourselves
and don't know it's going on
there's a lot of plays in the game
they range from the king to the pawn

the goals that we seek may be lofty
but the language we use leaves some doubt
that we understand the problem
or what we are talking about

if we would record all we say
and listen as it's played back
we'd say a lot less without thinking
and move on a smoother track

i wish

lots of things start with a wish
and a lot of wishes come true
the wish is really the thing
that it takes to make you do what you do

you can wish your whole life through
and never accomplish a thing
or get up and do what you have to
and have the things it will bring

the real you

i know you well
or i say i do
i watch as i
hear your voice
your face and manor
tell me much
as i search
to make a choice
smiles and frowns
can tell a lot
but they can cover too
and hide away
your inner self
and fool me as you do

all in how you think

i really don't know who said it
or if it was said at all
but i think i'll print it on this plaque
and hang it on the wall
it's the best advice i've heard of lately
it should be there to see-------------
"IF I TAKE CARE OF MY THINKING
MY THINKING WILL TAKE CARE OF ME"

please!

don't call attention to my faults
just to see me squirm
for that's exactly what it does
and pulls my nerves up firm

my innerself shouts - come fight back
my patience pleads - subdue
i'm out of balance with myself
and not too fond of you

i have my faults and know them well
i hate them each in turn
i know them well - hate them - loathe them
and the pain that they can earn

so please be kind and i'll be too
t'will save us both much pain
an each will lose at least one fault
the fact that we complain

163

so -

nothing came out of my head today
'couldn't get nothing to rhyme
i tried to think but it didn't work
i also had plenty of time

everything already seemed to be done
no matter how hard i tried
so i put my pen and paper away
and a poem that started just died

take it - don't leave it

most of my poems are full of advice
most that i should heed myself
most are things that have been told to me
and a lot are in the books on your shelf

don't make mistakes when knowledge is near
to neglect finding out would be sad
since life is made up of the best and the worst
get most of the best and be glad

i was thinking

all the bits of knowledge
that i've forced into my brain
shore up my quest to learn
all i can retain
i like to have my wits intact
and balance in my mind
as i face the challenge of the day
each day's one of a kind
some days it's force or wit
the store of knowledge
knows its stock
and give me facts to fit
an added fact retained today
will strengthen all tomorrow
and stand me in good stead once more
or shield me from some sorrows

just i love you

the depth of love
i feel for you
is as you wish it dear
the words seem most inadequate
to tell what you should hear
they should fill you with ecstasy
i really hope they do
cause there's lots of love and feeling
in every
i love you

everybody's different

everybody's different
so i am different too
now if we all are different
then, of course, it's true of you
i know you don't deny this
but you seem to press the point
yet, i don't know how this helps me
when my health is out of joint

sounds like

it's good that sound waves
need some things
to bring us all the news
and lots of other sounds
from many we can choose
with these systems men devise
they keep us well-informed,
smart, and very wise
i'd like to know what dogs hear
those things i've been denied
but doctors hear the babies laugh
while nestled there inside
if i could hear each word
while standing in a crowd
that would be unheard of
noisy and t-o-o loud

just think

i hate to just sit and stare into space
looking concerned with all things in place
to tell the truth i'm not thinking at all
i'm resting my head my brain's put on stall

my head needs a rest from the daily routine
to escape from it all it has heard and seen
well! here it comes back to it's normal state
i have to think now and i best not be late

let us pray

we send our prayers to the heavens high
way beyond the clear blue sky
we pray for problems here on earth
the spectrum spreads from death to birth
amass your problems near our door
we will pray, entreat, implore,
and ask the Lord to grant our plea
to set your mind and body free
we hope our humble posture here
brings father, son, and mother near
to hear us plead your case for you
we pray with all our strength they do

labor love

the first 12 days
of the month are gone
so have the
total hours
i raced and fought
worked real
hard
expending all
my powers
i chose and did
important things
left some undone
of course
i like to work
and do my thing
i win and lose
with force
i roll with punches
smile and try
i do it day by day
just give me once
a time to rest
from things i do - and say

at 75

in order to get
to seventy-five
you have to
cover much ground
otherwise you
won't be here
to have
a look around
the ground ain't
smooth
the hills get high
the valleys
sometimes gray
but the love
you lean on
will take you
all the way

laughing's okay, but

if you gotta be funny
please space out the fun
i'll laugh at the first joke
'til the next one's begun

i'll pay close attention
so my laugh is sincere
i'll be tickled to death
'til the laughter brings tears

i'll dwell on the punch line
and remember it well
and strive for the moment
when i can re-tell

i laugh each day
as much as i can
'cause i truly believe
it increases life's span

all else i must do
with the same force and zest
but to laugh all the time
causes pains in my chest

life's oscars

many are able
to run the show
but the chance
eludes them
enmasse
they have all the fists
they need to perform
ability - wisdom and class
they hurt in their hearts
but their heads
are held high
as time after time
life passes them by
they sharpen their wits
and practice their skills
work on their dream
cannot stop
they forge along
with relentless force
seeking a spot at the top -

"long and short of it"

some of our days are like minutes
some of our minutes like days
pressure squeezes time of work
pleasure pleads the moment stay
if the balance stays quite constant
you'll endure and reach your goal
minutes spent in too much trouble
weighs too heavy on one soul!

more than friendship

love is a friendship
that has caught on fire
it is sharing forgiving and true

it settles for less than perfection
makes allowances for
weaknesses too

love likes the present and future
forgets what is gone
and past

foster it kindly it's precious
it's <u>you</u> that can
make it last

words

the forces that effect our lives
are numerous in scope
they consist of words and phrases
with which we all must cope

we can resist the wind and wave
the tumult of the storm
protect ourselves from violence
and many kinds of harm

but words are devastating
crushing - harmful - bad
they cause untold depression
and leave us very sad

when you get the small talk over

when you get the small talk over
and there's nothing more to say
you wish for some conclusion
so you could be upon your way
not that there's some place to go
or task that you must do
but you know the other fellow
feels just about like you
there's that little hesitation
just before you part
when both of you would like to go
but neither wants to start

173

new - change - new

each generation has a way of its own

the way that they dress and their music's tone

there's an endless store for the new young crowd

who could have thought of music that loud

hair has replaced the old college beanie

girls swim and pose in a three ounce bikini

if they go past eighteen by not too far

they hurt to the core 'cause they don't have a car

their things at the store all cost too much

take blue jeans for instance now soft to the touch

well, i could go on but it's useless, you know

'cause the next bunch will come

with more "neat stuff" to show

steve

now you take steve
he's a pretty nice guy
he's a tad bit fresh
has a twinkle in his eye
he's up on things
like sports and news
his language is good
as are words he'd use
like i say, he's kindof fresh
but you won't mind that--
and he's thin and lean
quick as a cat
he holds his fork
a peculiar way
but he only does that
three times a day
with these kind words
i take my leave
i've had my fill --- !
now you take steve

next time around

if they let me come back
to mother earth
i'll do it again
for all it's worth
the time went by
lickety-split
i didn't have time
to rest or sit
always something going on
another day's gone
some were bad
but most were fun
but i liked them all
when it's said and done

now . . . . !

how can i tell with this paper and pen
that i'm well on the road to recovery again
i don't want to relive all those hours anew
i'm thankful to all that they're over and through
i want to tell "all" that their skills, love and prayers
proves once again that the world really cares.

no-yes

sometime
no or yes
is all you
have to say

it encompasses
the total
in the simplest
shortest way

there are
lots of words
to add to this
but it may
destroy the thing

and change
the total concept
it was really
meant to bring

the right thing

some times the choices are many
pulling and tugging with force
your mind says do this
then it says
you really can't do that
no - is the answer - of course
but if you do it you'll prosper
if not you will come up short
and you'll always have the memory
stuck in your aching heart
if you come out 50 - 50
after trying your very best
you'll cry and rejoice from decisions
even when you just guess

i raise my voice

i raise my voice - i scream and shout
i jump and kick til bones and muscles all give out
i tell the crowd "stand up and cheer"
that is why we all are here
my costume's cute...and i am too
but i'm a mess when i am through
the game is over
"we won the game"
but i will never be the same
i'd rather be a little neater
but i can't and be
a girl cheerleader

178

once upon a time

i think of my horse
almost every day
he comes to mind
in a pleasant way
i remember how
my hair would blow
the paths we took
and how fast we'd go
how he would react
to my gentle tug
and he'd know i was pleased
when my legs would hug
we could run away
down a dusty road
or walk along
where water flowed
we were friends
my horse and i
it's nice to recall
as days slip by!

valentine
1966

as i told you many years ago
that when our task is done
the job that took the two of us
has really made us one

although they have not reached us yet
the shadows do creep near
they force me even closer
and your presence is more dear

a few short days away from you
has reaffirmed anew
that i am blessed with
you my queen
and love that's good and true

lonesome?

if you are lonesome in a crowded room
and all you see all day is gloom

you'd better take a good hard look
down the road - the one you took

re-route yourself don't look for aid
for inside you the change is made!

the art of urination

the art of urination
all began with God's creation
and it fits in rather nice
with how we think
we want coffee, tea and beer
any liquid that is near
morning, noon and night
we love to drink
when in our complex system
our organs can resist them
and the liquid can be torture in disguise
if you can't relieve your bladder
nothing else on earth will matter
and lots of tears
will well up in your eyes

the ear

pay attention to all you hear
'cause knowledge comes as you listen
your eyes are placed on your head just so
and you learn except what you're miss'n
remember too to hear yourself
and learn from what you say
for other ears record your thoughts
that may never go away

"the thing"

do you ever feel like
"the thing" is too big
what is "the thing" you say

why, the "thing" is what
everything is about
as you live from day to day

it's the luck, and the slip
the good and the bad
that seems to come your way

so prepare for things
you cannot help
so you can fight and stay

the weight of wait

the weight of wait
is a bothersome thing
it fills you with thoughts
the impending will bring
you lose your control
to blank from your mind
inevitable happenings
the unpleasant kind
sometimes the effort to think with control
is enough to achieve the troublesome goal

the landlord

the light is out - my key is lost
the yard is full of junk folks tossed
the toilet's running over now
the air conditioner quit somehow
i will not sign next year's lease
i will not pay that big increase
the tax is none of my affair
there's no improvement anywhere
if i'd stay here i'd be a fool
who wants to office in a school
the hall is dirty - what should i do?
i cannot do it all myself
mop the floor - dust the shelf
fix the leaks - clean the room
i must get busy with the broom
i thought this job was just a snap
how does one - release this
<u>trap</u>

the price you pay

did you ever weigh
the price you pay
for your attitude
t'ward things?

if you must be right
you start a fight
with the grim results
it brings

if you let it go
and absorb the blow
it may be
saving grace

if end result
from the blow you felt
saved a friendship
hard replaced

this thing

i detect a tinge of something
that barricades my mind
an indefinable-a myth
of some uncertain kind

it stands guard with endless patience
holding me at bay
there is nothing i can really do
to make it go away

this thing has just one purpose
upon my mind to press
and make me ever conscious
of the price of happiness

let me off

let me off the merry-go-round
i've had enough fun for a while
let me recoup my senses
and live in a quiet style
let me sleep and rest in peace
with not a place to go
leave me be - to help myself
relax from head to toe
turn the music and lights down
while i lounge in a cool cool place
i'd like to do just nothing -
nothing but stare into space

we'll try

the number of times
you miss the boat
depends on the way
you keep it a-float

if you go in rough waters
with it's tail in the wind
you made two mistakes
and with caution you sinned

look ahead and be safe
avoid any storm
you will also avoid
the results of the harm

down the road

when i was very very young
i could not see where roads
would lead
like everyone i tried and guessed
somehow i knew i would succeed
just keep thinking that you're right
of course there's always doubt
goals are endless and forever
that's what this is all about

easy does it

you and i are in the same boat
we're trying our best to stay afloat
yet we bark at each other
and must have our way
we fuss and fret day after day
yet the goal we both seek
is near neck and neck
and we'll get there some day
if it kills us by heck
so be nice to your neighbor
and help him along
'cause you could <u>never</u> guess
what he's got going on!

it's over-but

when the whole thing's done and over
and the final dot is made
we reflect upon the happenings
by this our minds are swayed

soon we melt and mellow
choosing just the good
we bury once forever
all the things we should

for we must also pass the test
when our book is closed
charity is all that's left
except what heaven knows

we came before

we came before the man on the moon
before no clutch on the car
in fact the popular model T ford
had fenders hard to scar

there was not stuff like fiberglass
or plastic bags for junk
and if you took a train somewhere
the family took a trunk

folks would take a walk at dusk
without a thought of crime
the ice box had a block of ice
if the ice man came on time

the zipper was not heard of
mama wore a hat to church
the TV came much later
so the children did not curse

you could have bought the national league
not just the new york mets
for only one year's salary
that nolan ryan gets

the circus was the greatest place
that you could take a kid
he could dream forever after
about all the things they did

this could go on forever; i hate to quit so soon
but i have to go this minute - i've got a ticket to the moon!

what next

where do i stand in the sphere of time
what shall i do with this life of mine?
take the easy road safe to go
with no challenge no risk or pain to show
shall i stay in the fight with it's slings and bows
get up to the line with worthy foes
risk my neck, my cash, my health
to gain a little more of wealth
the action though it takes its toll
is exercise and feeds the soul

i was begot

i was begot and you were begot
and you will beget someone

we're a long way off from where we begun
the web is constantly being spun

i hope the millennium yet far off
will produce a clan with pride

then we'll congratulate each other
when in heaven we're side by side

"you ken the knew"

when we come face to face
on judgment day
with a judge who keeps track
of our earthly way
he'll point out the things
where we missed the boat
he'll have the record
quote for quote
when we say we did it
so and so
because we really did
not know
he'll tell us the answer
was in our reach
if we had listened
to what he preached
think it over while
there's still time -
to waste the chance
would be a crime!

imagine my friend

imagine my friend and i think you can
what would make a perfect man

he need not be smart as the world demands
but kind and refined with few demands

he would love with truth be fair to win
he would finish all he would begin

he would set a pace he could pursue
preserve his strength to see things through

his faith in all would make it so
he's steer a course to there he'd go

he'd make you love him by his deeds
he'd give respect to what succeeds

seek out his attributes perhaps just one
at least you will have then begun

win or lose

we are subjected to push and pull
to give and also to take
no matter how hard we try to do right
we will now and then make a mistake
it's fun to be in the game of life
tho' the penalties can be harsh
we cry when we lose, rejoice when we win
as we race through life with our torch!

yes or no

sometimes the answer's yes
sometimes the answer's no
'cause most of the time there's a question
about the way things will go
we sit on the brink of disaster
or play with our sorrows and joy
when we know life's a serious business
not a thing with which you can toy
it's true - yes or no can change things
to make us happy or sad
but the time that you wait for the answer
that's the thing that is really bad

that boy

He wants to be like his dad! You men,
Did you ever think, as you pause,
that the boy who watches your every move
is building a set of laws?
he's molding a life you're the model for,
and whether it's good or bad
depends upon the kind of example set
to the boy who'd be like his dad.

would you have him go everywhere you go?
have him do just the things you do?
and see everything that your eyes behold,
and woo all the gods you woo?
when you see the worship that shines in the eyes
of your lovable little lad,
could you rest content if he gets his wish
and grows to be like his dad?

it's a job that none but yourself can fill;
it's a charge you must answer for;
it's a duty to show him the road to tread
'ere he reaches his manhood's door.
it's a debt you owe for the greatest joy
on this earth to be had;
the pleasure of having a boy to raise
who wants to be like his dad!

your attitude

did you ever weigh the price you pay
for your attitude t'ward things

if you must be right you start a fight
with the grim results it brings

if you let it go and absorb the blow
it may be saving graced!

if the end result from the blow you felt
saved a friendship hard replaced

your enemy

the greatest enemy you have
is there inside of you
it's fear, distrust, and hate and doubt
that govern what you do
most everyone is much the same
if the truth were known
otherwise there'd be less pain
and more love would be shown
time slips by - the moment's gone
when we could change our ways
and lead a tranquil loving life
'til we run out of days

alone can't last

i ate at lloyd's - by myself
i slept in the bed - alone
the house lost its life - and beauty
in fact it was cold - as stone

my tools turned to things of torture
the yard was pretty - but sad
my shirts are at the laundry
i'm sure they'll come back - bad

i put too much soap in the washer
the dryer i had to run - trice
i did eat a little breakfast
but only had dinner twice

the world is full of people
i'm sure they're as good as they look
but life is a drag at best
unless i spend it with - snook

another season

another season has come and gone
the crack of the bat
and the smell of popcorn, beer, and hot dogs
has been blown south by the chill north winds
the sweat has been removed from the uniforms
gloves are folded in half
and the signatures are well stained into the balls
that rest on the desks and mantels across our land
what of the people -
I know one who missed his first season in many years
his scrap book closed a few weeks before last season

you are what you are

you are what you are
'cause you do what you do
and the same is true in reverse

so watch yourself as you act out life
and take out
what makes you worse

don't say it

a wise man said
to bite your tongue
he did not mean it you know

he meant don't finish
the sentence - or your
friend will turn into foe

a few misplaced words
can work havoc and
throw your life in a spin

so bite your tongue
and button your lip or
your world may start crumbling in

mechanical things

mechanical things are easy for me
things put together - now that i can see

but folks can stand there and talk all day
and leave me as confused as i can be

things stay together in a nice array
but words sometimes can slip away!

198

Mr. Water

take a glass and go to the sink
and contemplate this before you drink
ken kifer works hard hours on end
so the faucet gives agua from our nice agua friend
when you sing in the shower, sing his praises and more
and turn off your sprinklers, if he comes to your door
he's such a nice guy. . . let's do all we can
to show we appreciate our fine H2O man

queen of hearts

a woman can make a full house
and can win all as Queen of Hearts
she can hold a flush with all of
it's intrical parts
she can fill a straight with a Jack
and never expose her hand
she can bid with awful high stakes
and win just as if it was planned
the Dealer can never defeat her
she has a much stronger will
but it all is all very simple
she has much more in life to fill

some folks seem

some folks seem to never forget
'cause <u>you</u> think with the mind
that ain't wore out yet
today I'll get knowledge
and store it away
--now where did I put it?
what did you say--?

start over

i would like to write some things
about the tongue
and what it can express
it can raise you to the greatest heights
or fill your world with stress
it can send the notes of music
to the pinnacle of sound
it can hold back information
that never can be found
it can send you down a path in life
where you should never be
it can send you on a journey
and fill your life with glee
all speech produced by silver tongues
may not be pure as gold
cause sometimes they just have to say
well that's what i've been told

i started at 7 A.M.

i started at 7 A.M. to talk
of course i listened too
but all of those words sure added up
it came to quite a few

i do the same thing everyday
and when the day is done
i must have heard and said a bunch
since talking i begun

the gift

the gift you get is the gift you earn
the way you earn it i discern
it's given with no strings attached
the gift and deed are seldom matched
the thing you did aroused my joy
a moment nothing can destroy
i gave the gift to let you know
you pleased me and it needs to show
accept this gift i bring to you
it helps me have my joy a new.

bliss

ignorance - is bliss?
that hardly makes good sense
everything that you should know
sometimes is your defense
so if "you don't know nothing"
about the thing at hand
how can nothing help you
when you must take a stand?
of course there's always silence
to substitute for fact
and the audience may never know
if your talent is to act

the curious

never a day can come and go
that the curious do not learn
curious does not mean you're smart
but attentive and have concern
the curious ask "what if" and "why"
and switch and turn "the thing"
to hunt for something different
and results that is might bring
the curious are persistent
seeking something new
they create from something old
this gives life, zest and reason
to most of what they do!

no ticket

i used to buy a ticket
so i'd be entertained
i came away with little
and a little i retained
so now i just observe things
that are going on around
often it is just a glance
or maybe it's a sound
there's a mighty million -
of things to be observed
to please or bring you pleasure
or by pressure that it served
you don't have to buy a ticket
to see joy in children's eyes
or to listen to a rooster crow
when the sun begins to rise
lots is going on around
to watch and hear all day
to fill you full of joy and hope
as each day fades away.

september 19, 1985

today's a climax in my life
now let me make it clear
snook said i'm looking better
and today i had a beer

now do not take this lightly
'cause a main event occurred
my system welcomed back the beer
and not a better word was heard

listen!

we listen for things with keen persistence
that may change or effect our whole existence
somethings deplete us to an empty shell
and plunge our hope to a bottomless well
while others soar us to limitless heights
and we bathe in the joy of their pleasing delights
the up - the down - the high - the low
the challenge to ride the tide and flow
the tears - the smiles - hate and devotion
stimulate the weak emotion
sharpens knowledge for making plans
strengthens one for life's demand

fish?
yes fish

to look at the lake with the naked eye
you'd never guess what just swam by
why - the whole thing moves with every size fish
the small one is always the bigger one's dish
unless - the big one meets bad fate
then the little ones come to clean that plate

the whole thing's done right by the book
but one thing's missing and that's the hook
now - the hook is the thing that the sportsmen use
to give the fish a bad case of blues
right there stops his carefree life
he's skinned alive with the sportsman's knife
he's split in half and loses his belly
and often the sportsman's name if Kelly

don't miss it

don't miss the drama
that's going on
don't let it go by
through neglect
don't let the sun
just come up or down
look out and get
the affect
another daily occurrence
that presents itself
by the minute
is a smile you receive
or give away
with the friendly message
within it
let's watch for tears
and the meaning they send
be it sorrow or joy
we can share
you don't have to do
a single thing
just look like
you mean it
and be there

everything changes

the grass now grows
where the tree once grew
the logs it made
have gone up the flue

the branch that
held the birds and squirrels
could be a stick
that some kid twirls

the grass is pretty
and the shade is gone
but the kid has fun
and the birds sing on

the squirrels have young
in other tress
and things are again
as nice as you please

hard to do

they talk about things
that are hard to make
like lenses and crystal
easy to break

towers of steel
that reach to the sky
a rocket that probes
since they taught it to fly

balloons full of water
on which you can sleep
a digital thing
that will count your sheep

a clock with no wheels
and no hands on its face
a weapon that shoots
some stuff they call mace

cameras that stop
the hummingbird's wings
dolls that can tinkle
and a robot that sings

but the human mind
with all it possesses
can't make up it's mind
to solve its own messes

i have to follow my own star

i cannot be like
anyone else
i have to follow
my star
i follow each path
in life as it comes
it worked out fine
so far

when i hurt
i hurt to the core
when i'm sad
i'm as sad as can be
when i'm happy
i show it
will all my force
so anyone can see

if you watch my face
as you talk to me
you'd know I understand
that what you say
is important to you
and that's what
you want me to see

come again?

now the thing
that's not done
must get done
to just think
that it ain't
ain't no fun
if you mentally
do it and do it
what you're doing
will not get done
so do the thing
that takes action
and get it out
of the way
so you can think
of that other thing
that you didn't do
yesterday
now come on -
get with it!
and do it -
there is no other way

he--awes
he--aus the world

to mrs. aus he is the world
and he's the world to me
just like the world in most respects
let's analyze and see

he's constantly upon the spin
and slightly tilted too
his top is white his ways are set
yet always in a stew

his center is the equator
volcanic, full of gas
monsoons of medicine to drench
this ever tortured mess

his mind and body can't agree
for constantly they spar
to folks that are not close to him
he shines like any star

just be you

i'm tired of pretending
i'm somebody else
i think i'm just gonna be me
i'll try it a while
and check the results
and see how much
change it will be
if i've done it too long
that i'm too far gone
i'll stay as i am and i doubt
that folks will even detect at all
just what it is i'm about
'cause you see no one paid much attention
all the time i was acting the part
i could have been me for all of that time
and not kidded myself from the start

i ain't been around

i ain't been around for a little while
i see that curls your little smile
you know i'm frail and bound to break
there's just so much my "bod" can take
so please do practice round the clock
you must be sharp when i need you doc

i do

some day the sun will rise
upon a world that's clean and free
what memories i am starting
for days that are to be
i'll tell my little spaniards
of the planes i helped make
i'll dream of spars and stringers
while i bake a birthday cake
as i wrap the school day lunch
i'll think of wrapping parts
the stories of my sweet entails
should warm my young one's hearts
i'm glad that i can do my bit
to help to beat the foe
i'm glad to know that this is not
as far as it will go
our pets will know their mom and dad
were there to lend a hand
to help make a peaceful place
for them upon this land

guiding light

i used to do a lot of things
i still do and i'm glad
i'm pretty good at what i do
and all the jobs i've had
nothing that i did was great
kinda middle of the road
but i reaped a mighty harvest
from the seeds i sowed
i have direct descendants
of every shape and kind
all are good to look at
strong of body - sharp of mind
you add to that
my charming wife
the darling of the clan
it all turns out
just dandy
for a very lucky man

the things that happen to me

i'm prone to blame others for causing
the things that happen to me
but i wink at myself in the mirror
for there it is plain to see
that the fellow that causes me trouble
is making a dunce out of me

little by little

it's the little by little
done day after day
accomplished - over a span
that gets results - better
than energy spent
known as
"flash in the pan"

thanks

thank you people
of long ago
your past left
more than you
could know
the wheel was great
it still serves well
as does the comb
and oil well
the camera too
is nice to have
so' aspirin
and mentholatum
salve
i can't leave out
the rocking chair
the baby bed
or rocking horse
or teddy bear
and all the things
i use each day
and have used
many years
so thank you
thank you thank you
you all deserve
three cheers

down but not out

down but not out
is a sequel in life
courted with by all
who exist

a few get by
the easy way
with a bump here and there
or maybe a slap on the wrist

a lot is blamed on what we eat
no exercise and such
but tension torment, lack of love
contribute all or much

you can't get by
with a scratch or two
life has too many flaws

18262 days

when the sun set darkens early
and the kids all move away
when the grandkids call you "nicknames"
and you smile at ways they play
when your glasses
hurt your nose and ears
and your old things still look new
and sunday comes so often
and you look for things to do
well - it went so fast
and now it's here
it's hard to hold back joyful tears-
to think that we've been married
for fifty happy years

eighty

you have to
do a lot of things
to get from
there to here
they say to
look ahead
with courage
hope - not fear
the days will come
and go again
just like they
did before
they say do some thing
new each day
and you'll enjoy
them more
to do the same
thing over
will only spin your wheels
i think i'll follow
their advice
and see what it reveals

not bad

i've been over and out
and up and down
i've been back and forth
and in
i've seen many a thing
get finished
and some that could not begin

i have wailed at the tomb
and laughed at myself
i've been bitter and
pleasantly sweet
i've been mighty cold
and drenched in sweat
in all but unbearable heat

but i never felt as i came along
that the world had treated me bad
'cause most of the days were full of joy
and only a few were sad

i'll be seeing you

i cannot reach you
where you are
why did you leave
and go so far
i had things i'd like to say
if you had stayed
for one more day
i'd just say things
i have always said
but now they're locked up
in my head
i would like to hug you tight
to look down in your eyes
to hear you whistle
"stardust" - and children's
lullabies
i could go on but i must wait
'til we meet - at heaven's gate

my mind has restful caverns

my mind has restful caverns
where from time to time i go
it's my retreat from trials i meet
'bout things i do not know

the daily tasks i must perform
i accomplish in my stride
i understand and i can do
most everything i've tried

but some things i don't know at all
they truly baffle me
that when i just stare in space
i only look but do not see

the dust of time

the dust of time is made of things
ground fine in life's great mill
respect it as you blow it from
off the windowsill

they say there's nothing new at all
that things just change with time
a particle of dust in space
was once the ocean's slime

the dust of human ashes
must spill from every urn
so the shell that holds the precious you
can to the earth return

about poets

everything i've done
'til now
has brought me
to this place
i hope that
when i leave you
there's a smile
on every face
i'll remember
all your faces
and the things
that we said here
and hope they'll come
to mind for you
in poems
year by year